I WILL NOT DIE
ALONE

BOOKS BY DERA WHITE

I Will Not Die Alone

**BOOKS ILLUSTRATED BY
JOE BENNETT**

I Will Not Die Alone

*A Bathroom Book
for People Not Pooping or Peeing
but Using the Bathroom as an Escape*

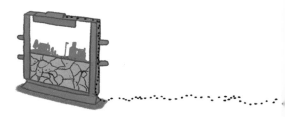

I WILL NOT DIE ALONE

written by
DERA WHITE
illustrated by
JOE BENNETT

A TOM DOHERTY ASSOCIATES BOOK
NEW YORK

This is a work of fiction. All of the characters, organizations, and events portrayed in this novel are either products of the author's imagination or are used fictitiously.

I WILL NOT DIE ALONE

A Forge Book
Published by Tom Doherty Associates
120 Broadway
New York, NY 10271

www.tor-forge.com

Forge® is a registered trademark of Macmillan Publishing Group, LLC.

The Library of Congress Cataloging-in-Publication Data
is available upon request.

ISBN 978-1-250-76043-2 (hardcover)
ISBN 978-1-250-76044-9 (ebook)

Our books may be purchased in bulk for promotional, educational, or business use. Please contact your local bookseller or the Macmillan Corporate and Premium Sales Department at 1-800-221-7945, extension 5442, or by email at MacmillanSpecialMarkets@macmillan.com.

First Edition: October 2021

Printed in China

0 9 8 7 6 5 4 3 2 1

I WILL NOT DIE
ALONE

I WILL NOT DIE ALONE.

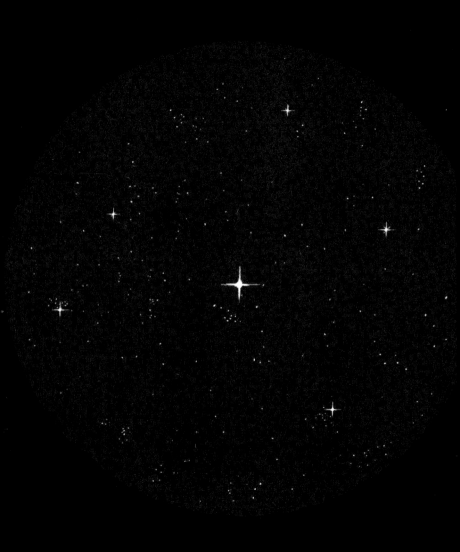

MY LIMITATIONS WILL NOT GET IN
THE WAY OF MY PASSIONS.

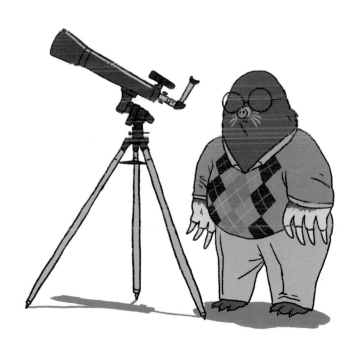

I FIND BEAUTY IN ORDINARY THINGS.

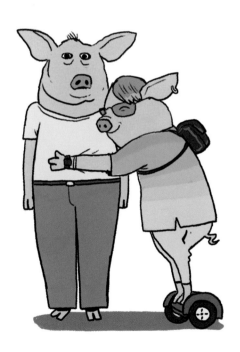

MY BODY IS STRONG AND MY MIND IS SHARP.

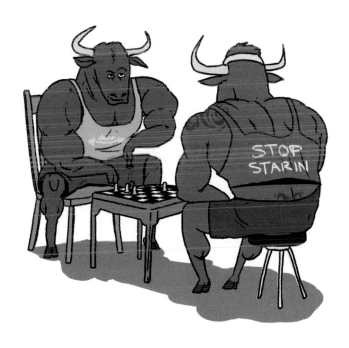

ONE DAY, IT'LL ALL COME TO ME.

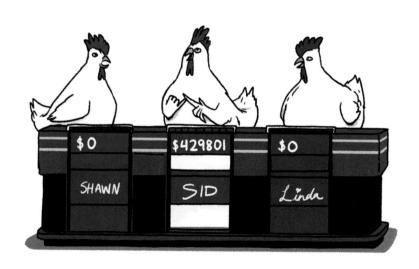

I AM YOUNG AT HEART.

MY SEXIEST YEARS ARE AHEAD OF ME.

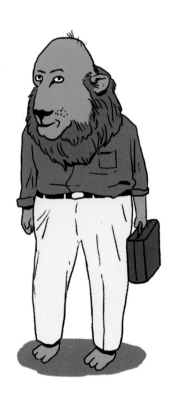

I WILL PUT TURMERIC IN EVERYTHING.

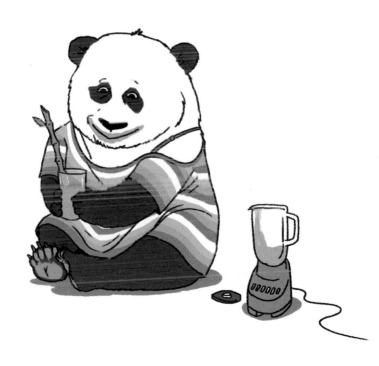

I WILL LET GO OF ALL
DISEMPOWERING BELIEFS.

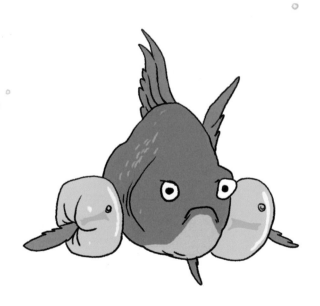

WORRY IS UNIVERSAL.

WebMD
SWEATING A LOT?
POSSIBLE CONDITIONS
· CANCER
· DIABETES
· CANCER AGAIN

I WILL REMEMBER TO
TAKE THE TRASH OUT.

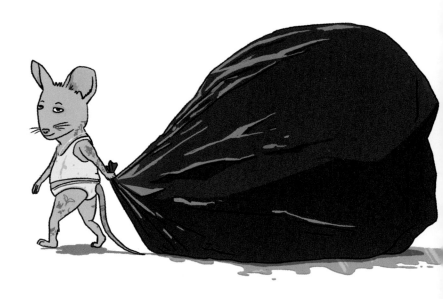

I WILL SURROUND MYSELF
WITH THE LOVE OF MY ANCESTORS.

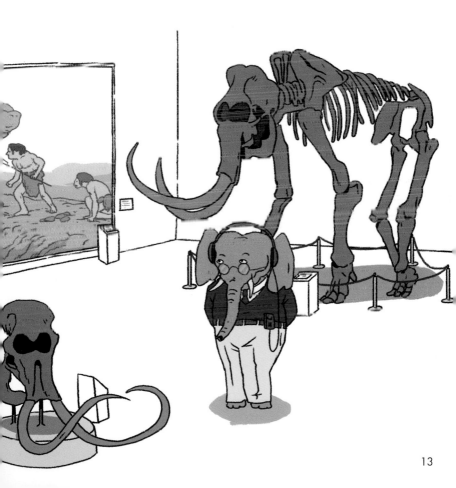

I WILL LIMIT MY DAILY SCREEN TIME.

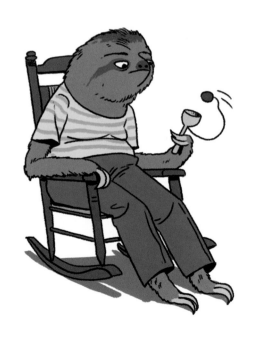

I WILL INSTEAD PUT EFFORT INTO
MAKING THE PEOPLE AROUND ME FEEL GOOD.

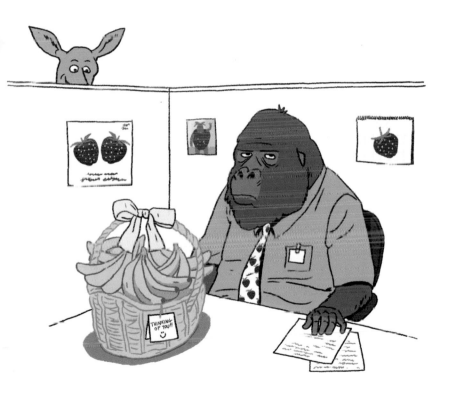

MY SUCCESS IS IN MY HANDS.

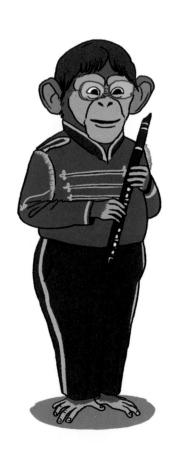

POSITIVE THINKING
FEELS NATURAL TO ME.

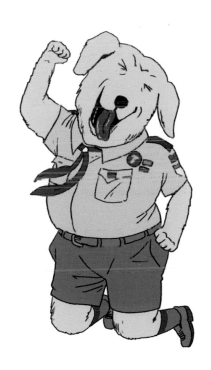

I WILL LET GO
WHEN THE MOMENT CALLS FOR IT.

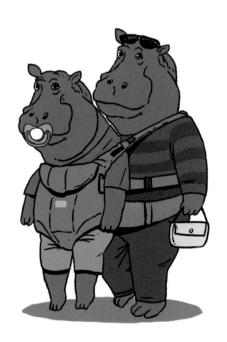

I AM A STRONG WOMAN,
AND I TRUST MY BODY.

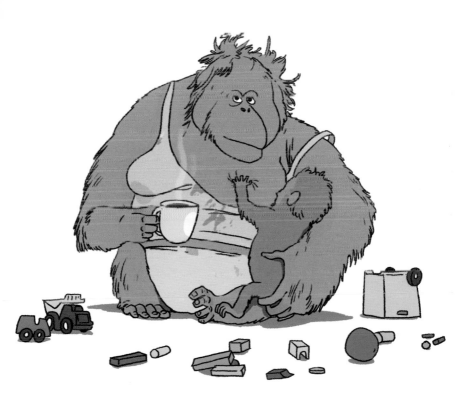

WE ALL HAVE FLAWS AND THAT'S OKAY.

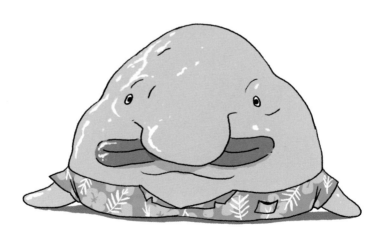

Woah.

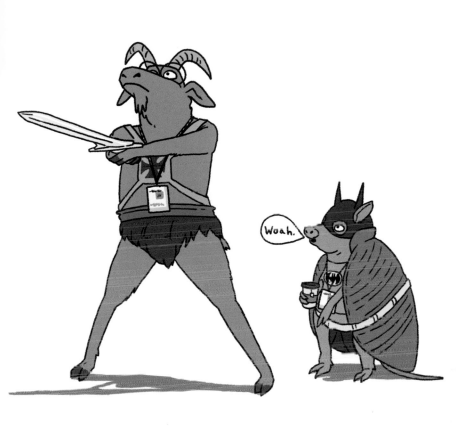

I WILL BELIEVE.

MY VOICE WILL BE HEARD.

LINDA!!!!!
LINDA

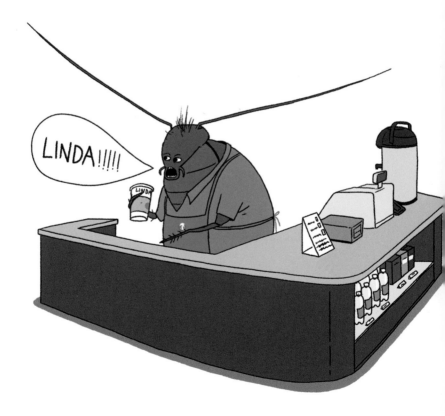

I WILL BUY LESS COFFEE OUT
AND MAKE MORE COFFEE AT HOME.

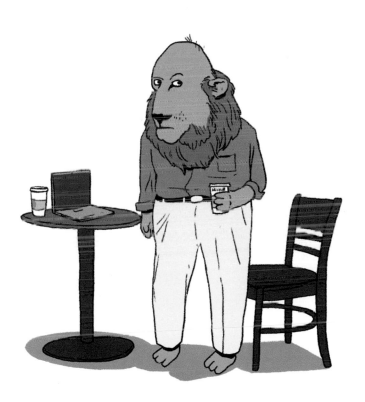

THE MOM JEANS TREND HAS ALLOWED
ME SO MUCH FREEDOM.

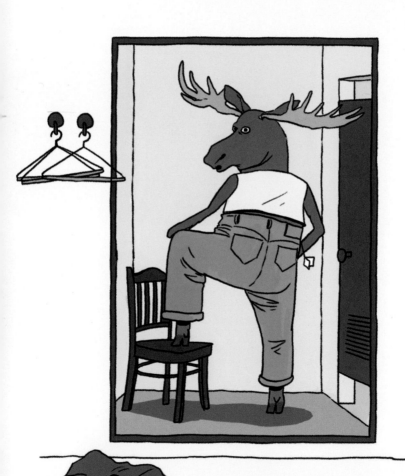

I AM AN UNMOVABLE MOUNTAIN,
WATCHING SEASONS COME AND GO.

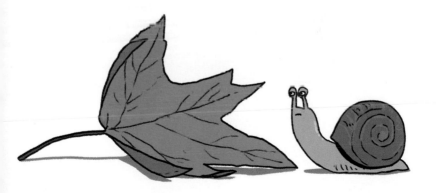

I AM LOOKING AT HER,
NOT THE TV BEHIND HER.

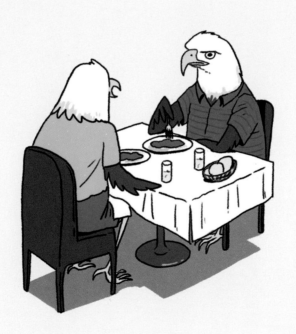

GIVING UP IS NOT AN OPTION TODAY.

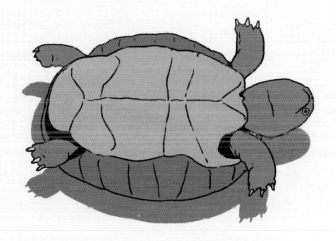

I AM ENOUGH.

I'M GOING TO EAT THIS
LIKE NO ONE IS WATCHING.

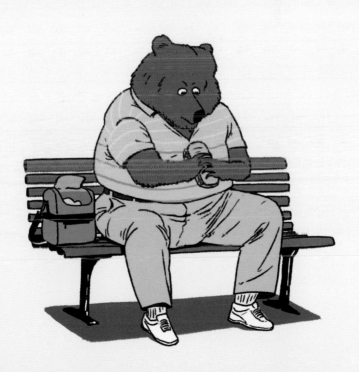

I CAN LEAVE THE HOUSE AT LEAST ONCE AND CONSIDER IT A PRODUCTIVE MONTH.

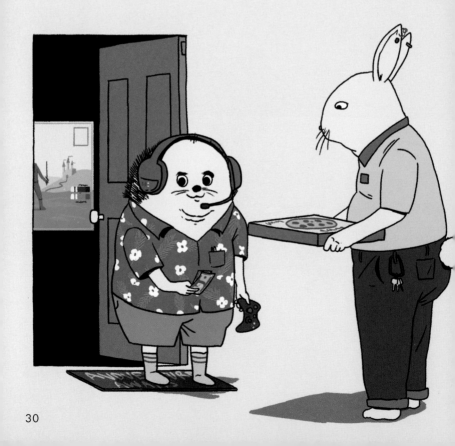

I WILL SURRENDER TO THE THINGS
IN LIFE THAT ARE OUT OF MY CONTROL.

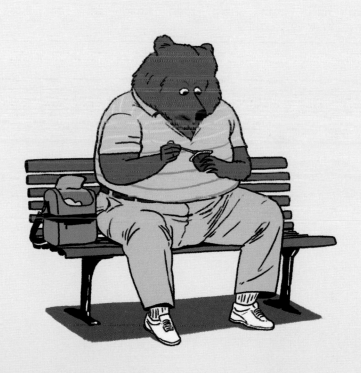

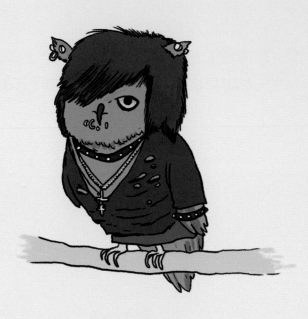

I JUST FEEL THINGS MORE
THAN A NORMAL PERSON.

I WILL TAKE TIME TO BE STILL.

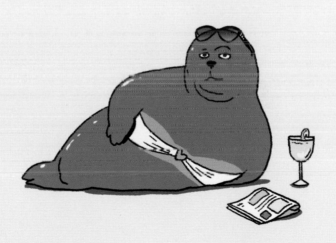

MONEY WILL NOT SOLVE ALL MY PROBLEMS.

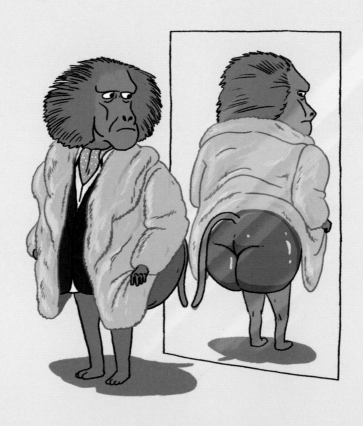

I NEED NO ONE ELSE'S APPROVAL.

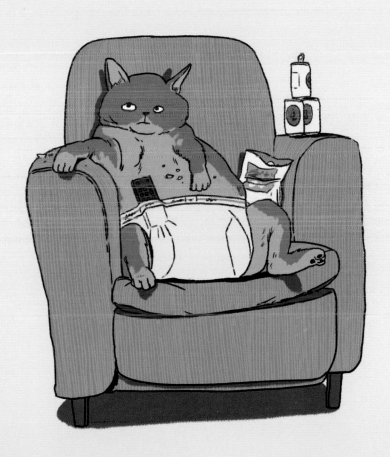

I WILL CARE FOR ALL CREATURES,
BIG AND SMALL.

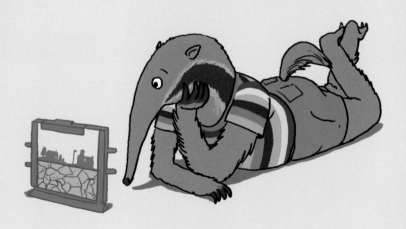

I WILL REACH NEW HEIGHTS.

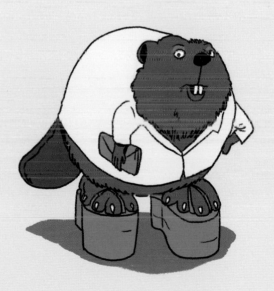

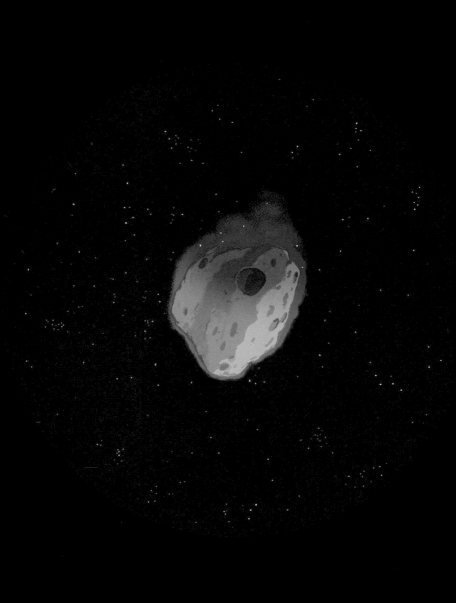

I WILL NOT COWER
IN THE FACE OF THE TRUTH.

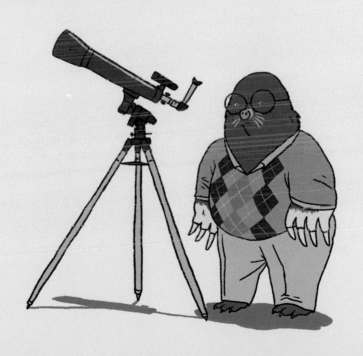

I WILL SPREAD AWARENESS...

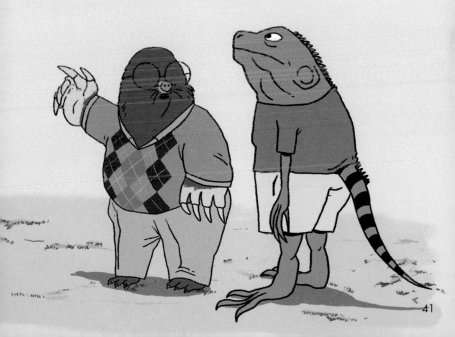

...AND EXTEND MY KNOWLEDGE...

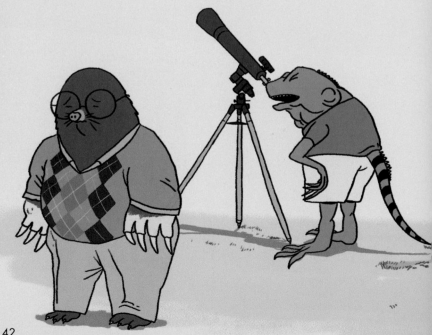

...AND CRY IN SUITABLE SITUATIONS.

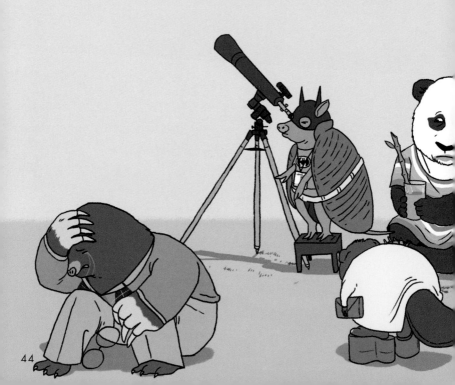

45

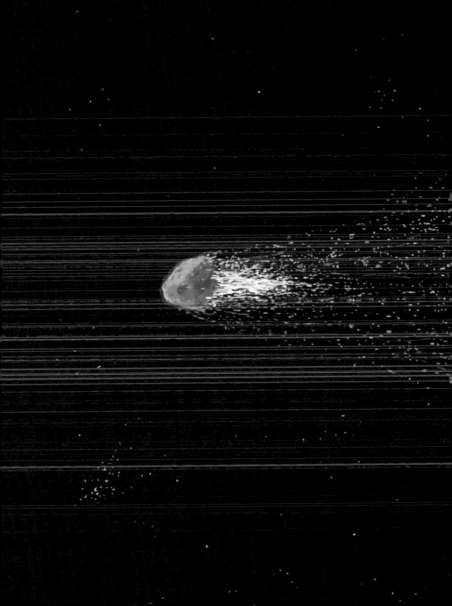

I WILL MAKE TIME FOR THE PRESENT.

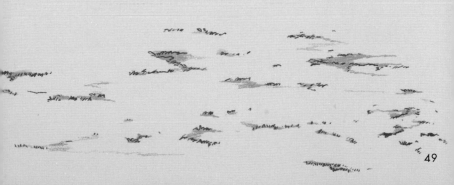

AND TAKE TIME TO BE SILENT...

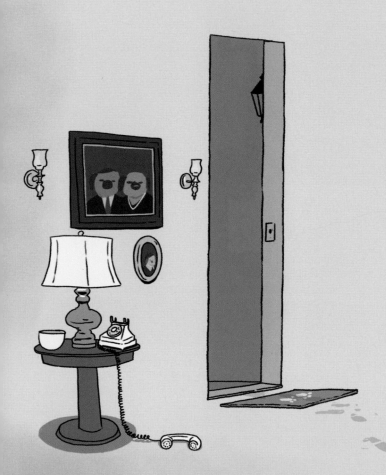

. . . .

. . . .

I AM CALM.

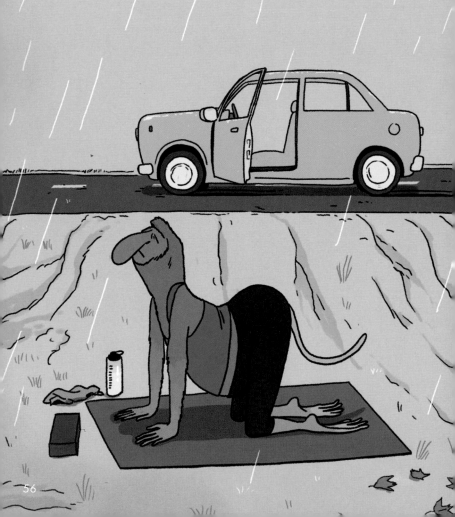

TIME IS ONLY AN ILLUSION.

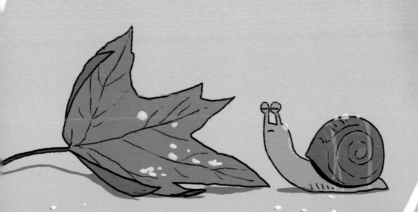

I WILL BREATHE.

BREAKING NEWS

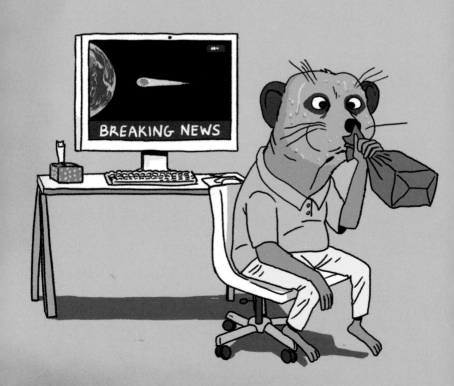

I AM NOT AFRAID.

WILL YOU MARRY ME

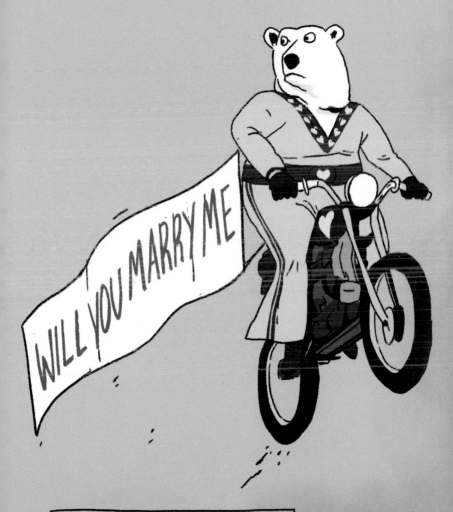

TODAY IS A NEW BEGINNING.

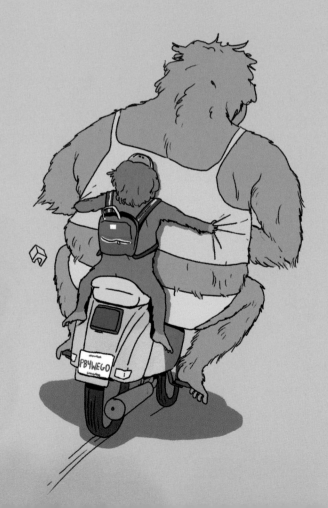

I WILL TURN MY PAIN INTO JOY.

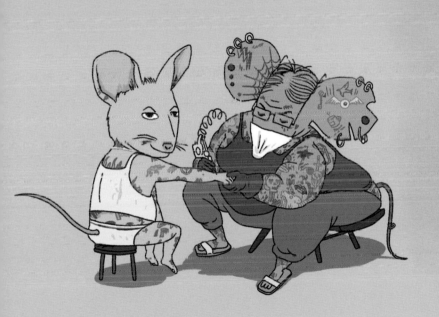

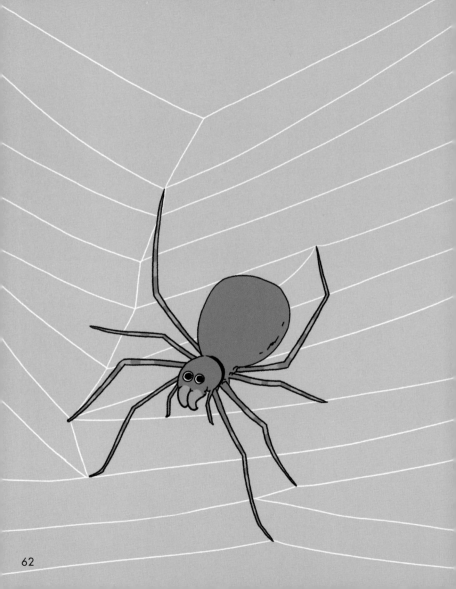

MY WORDS WILL BE MY CONTRIBUTION.

ITS BEEN REAL

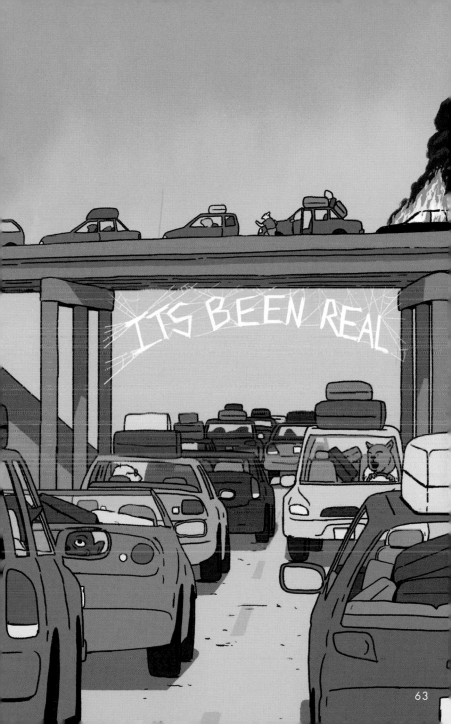

IF I PAUSE LONG ENOUGH,
I WILL NOTICE THE BEAUTY THAT SURROUNDS ME.

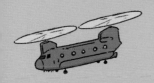

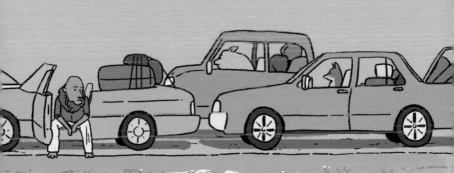

I WILL REASSESS THE VALUE OF MY COLLECTIBLES.

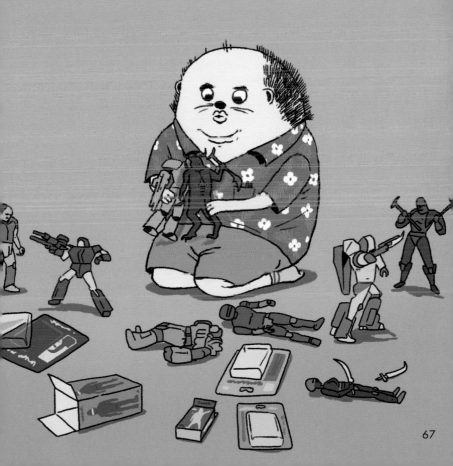

I WILL GIVE BACK WHERE I CAN.

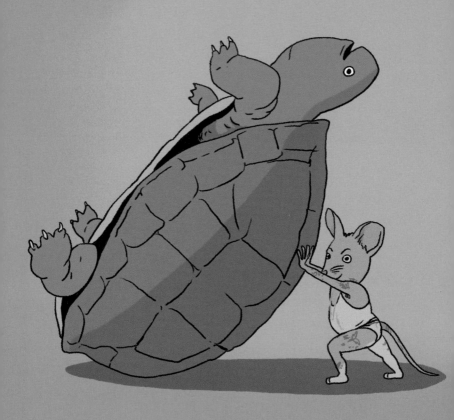

I'M DESERVING OF INDULGENCES.

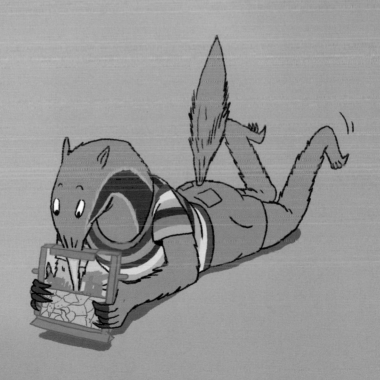

I WILL PERFECT MY CRAFT.

I WILL LEARN TO LIVE AGAIN.

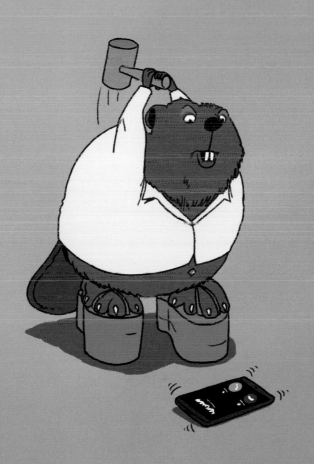

I WILL INVEST IN HAPPINESS.

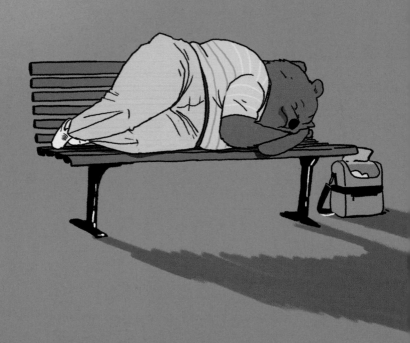

I WILL CHERISH EVERY
GREETING CARD I'VE RECEIVED.

I WILL LIVE WITH RECKLESS ABANDON.

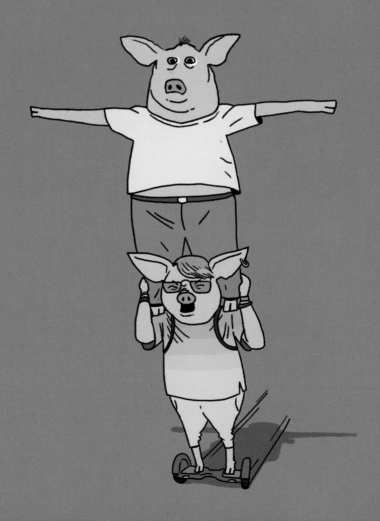

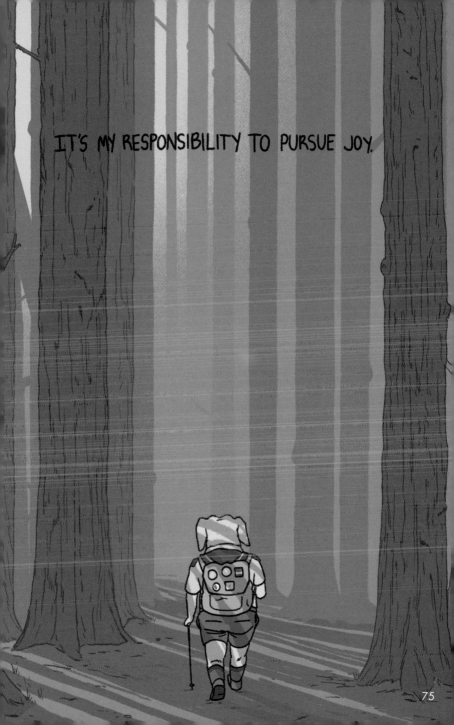

IT'S MY RESPONSIBILITY TO PURSUE JOY.

THIS SONG WON'T SING ITSELF.

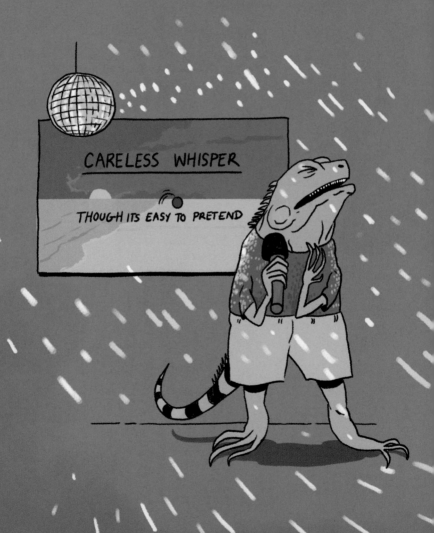

CARELESS WHISPER

THOUGH ITS EASY TO PRETEND

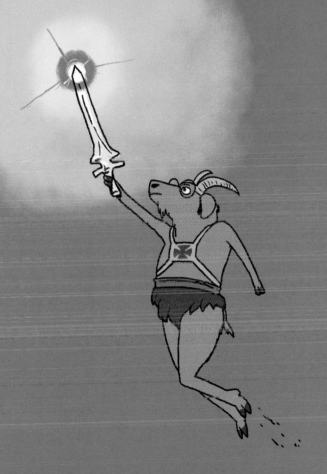

I AM THE MASTER OF MY UNIVERSE.

I WILL EMBRACE UNCERTAINTY.

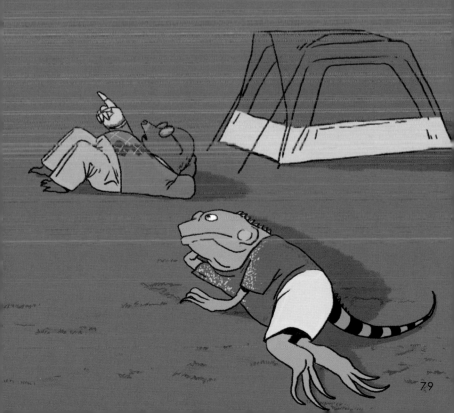

HARK!
WELCOME
SHOES OFF AT DOOR
AWAITS
THANK YOU

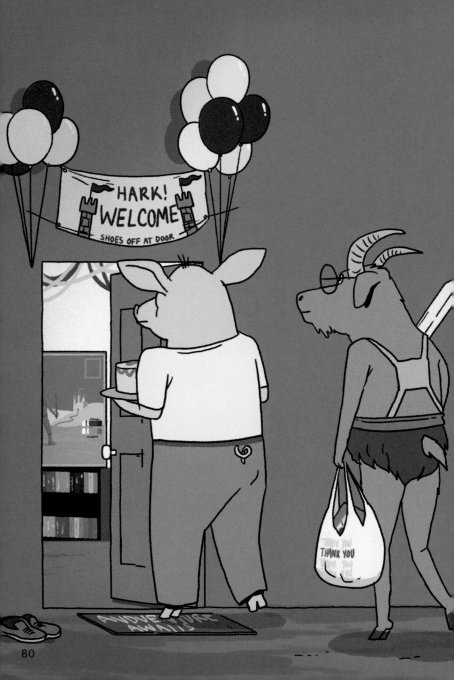

I WILL BROADEN MY COMFORT ZONE.

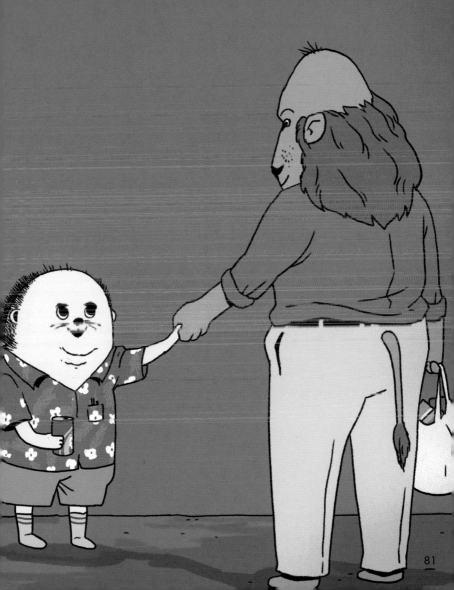

I SEE MYSELF

IN OTHERS.

I WILL NEVER IGNORE

84

ANOTHER SUNSET.

I WILL NEVER PASS UP
AN OPPORTUNITY TO LOVE.

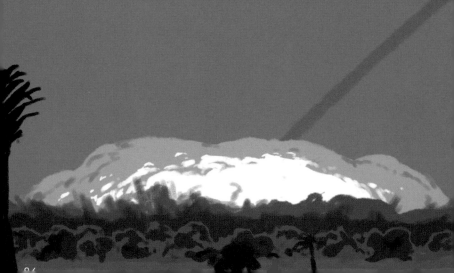

I WILL NOT DIE ALONE.

ACKNOWLEDGMENTS

MOM & DAD
TERRY WHITE
CAITLIN DÍAZ
NATHAN HEMSTRA
SEAN BUCKELEW
LISA MIERKE
KRISTIN TEMPLE
ALI FISHER
MEREDITH MILLER
LILY DOLIN
LINDA QUINTON
FRITZ FOY
TOM DOHERTY
JENNIFER McCLELLAND-SMITH
EILEEN LAWRENCE
ALEXIS SAARELA
SARAH REIDY
LUCILLE RETTINO
RYAN JENKINS
STEVEN BUCSOK
HEATHER SAUNDERS
KATIE KLIMOWICZ

ABOUT THE ILLUSTRATOR

JOE BENNETT is an artist and filmmaker living in Pasadena. He's made original work for FX, FOX, MTV, Comedy Central, and Adult Swim. He is the illustrator of *A Bathroom Book for People Not Pooping or Peeing but Using the Bathroom as an Escape* by Joe Pera.

Instagram: joe_bennett_animation

ABOUT THE AUTHOR

DERA WHITE is a writer and photographer best known for the You Are My Wild photo project. A native of Fairburn, Georgia, she continues to work and live in a suburb outside of Atlanta with her husband, Terry, and three daughters, Fiona, Neve, and Frances. *I Will Not Die Alone* is her debut.

Instagram: derafrances